HOW TO HEAL

FROM

Sophisticated Slavery

DONNA KAY HARRIS &

LETICIA LATRICE BARRETT

AuthorHouse™
1663 Liberty Drive
Bloomington, IN 47403
www.authorhouse.com
Phone: 1 (800) 839-8640

Published by AuthorHouse 03/07/2018

ISBN: 978-1-5462-3175-2 (sc)
978-1-5462-3189-9 (hc)
978-1-5462-3176-9 (e)

Print information available on the last page.

This book is printed on acid-free paper.

authorHOUSE®

Dedication

I dedicate this book to Jesus –

my Lord and my God, my Savior and best love I have ever known.

I have never felt so blessed, protected, and special until I let the love God enter my life.

Wherever you lead me I will follow and spread the word of God to everyone I meet.

What an honor to be a child of God.

Thank you.

Acknowledgements

I have been blessed to have an awesome family of elders.

Ethel Solomon and Pete Solomon (Fort Valley, GA) were my grandparents. They took care of our family in times of hardships. We lived with them and went to school in Georgia for a short period of time for protection.

Gladys Dawson, my aunt was the protector of our family during hard times. She was the Black Santa that always gave to me unconditional love and presents.

My Aunt Mae Harris was the spiritual Goddess in the family. I watched and learned how to honor God from her examples.

Mrs. Margaret Lee had the home that shared love to everyone in the community. She made sure when I was in her home I was cared for like a special child of God.

Mrs. Susie Harris, my aunt that treated me like a daughter.

As a reminder of love and support of my elders. I have a picture of these elders at work on my desk, and at home. I want to honor and remember all they taught me, and the love of God they shared with me.

Table of Contents

Introduction

Many African Americans are not aware of the dysfunctional behavior that may have resulted from the trauma their ancestors suffered in slavery. We all know the many common horror stories from slavery. However, many are not aware of the harmful effects it still has on our community to this day.

This book will not focus on the problems, but solutions. It is important for African Americans to be aware of the unhealthy behavior they have adopted and create ways to heal and move forward for the generations to come. The goal is to pass on a happy, healthy, and positive legacy. We need to pass on generational blessings, not curses. The African American community has suffered long enough. The time for change is now, but the change has to begin with you first.

Thankfully we are no longer in shackles or on the plantation, therefore we call the slavery we face today *sophisticated slavery*. It is very subtle, subliminal and often comes in the form of micro-aggressions. The many racist, strategic tactics were created to have multi-generational effects on the African American community. There were psychological strategies used to create dysfunctional behavior. These tactics were used to manipulate and mentally control the black community.

This book will discuss critical issues that are negatively affecting the African American race, as well as provide solutions on how to manage the pain, stress and anger. The book will provide positive methods for healing and moving forward to get to a healthy place. If every African American can individually change their behavior, take the time to heal, the entire African American race can be healed as a whole. The old saying goes "united we stand, divided we fall." Individually you have to heal from sophisticated slavery in order to move forward as a community.

This book is separated into topics that were identified as major issues affecting the African American community. One of the important ways to heal from sophisticated slavery is to shine light on major issues. This book is created as a journal to help you be introspective about the issues that are affecting you. The book encourages you to choose your method of healing through personal introspection, talking to a friend, a counselor, a spiritual minister of your choice or a psychologist.

The goal of this book is to help you on your journey to healing from sophisticated slavery. A special section in the book is created to show other cultures how they can assist in the healing process.

Tools For Everyone To Participate In Healing From Sophisticated Slavery

Past Slavery – versus – new Sophisticated Slavery and ways everyone can help with the healing process.

"Slavery *is, (according to Webster's dictionary) in the strictest sense of the term, any system in which principles of property law are applied to people, allowing individuals to own, buy and sell other individuals, as a de jure form of property. A slave is unable to withdraw unilaterally from such an arrangement and works without remuneration. Many scholars now use the term chattel slavery to refer to this specific sense of legalized, de jure slavery. In a broader sense, however, the word slavery may also refer to any situation in which an individual is de facto forced to work against their own will. Scholars also use the more generic terms such as unfree labor or* forced labour *to refer to such situations. However, and especially under slavery in broader senses of the word, slaves may have some rights and protections according to laws or customs. Slavery began to exist before written history, in many cultures. A person could become a slave from the time of their birth, capture, or purchase."*

How past slavery looked - major systems were enforced. From our perspective the major past slavery occurred and controlled 4 Spiritual Systems.

1. Family System

2. Financial System

3. Health Care System

4. Prison System

This book will demonstrate the years of aftermath and how it is affecting us still today. The new ways to help heal the world are no longer in the hands of the White House, politicians or the Slave owner. With current killings and natural disasters it is important for everyone to take a leadership role in healing this world. There are several ways everyone including Caucasian, Asian, and any other race(s) can participate.

This starts with how to heal from sophisticated slavery with a change in mental and spiritual energy. This process starts with a win/win attitude. We will start the healing process with 13 major steps towards healing that everyone can participate in.

1. The first step will be to drop the words of Superiority and White privilege, status and titles that we all hear all over the world. Moving toward everyone is equal and no one is better than the next human being beside you at work, home or in your community.

2. It is time for all human beings to take ownership of our behavior. Wrong policies and procedures that hinder a person's basic rights, health care and benefits should be equal for all people, no matter what age, handicap, pre-existing health condition you have, or what nationality you are.

3. Communication that is not supportive of all people leads to negative outcomes. By learning how to conduct meetings and healthy communications about barriers that exist helps us heal from sophisticated slavery. Plan 'meet and greets' in a forum that is positive and heals our spirit and soul with understanding of our differences. People are afraid to have honest communications with people that are different from themselves. However, that is the only way we share and grow from our differences to learn from one another. Fear of the unknown and the color of other human beings are big barriers that should be removed for our healing to begin.

4. Achieving humility is a great accomplishment to spiritual healing for everyone. Being honest about others being treated differently is a big part of healing.

5. Know your history and what your ancestors did to hinder or help heal from sophisticated slavery.

6. Forgiveness is a key factor toward healing sophisticated slavery. Forgiveness is important when a person is being introspective of what role they or their ancestors played in past slavery. This is a major role in healing to start shaping your heart and spirit toward the way you want your future to look for the next generations.

7. Change in perspective is key. We should be aware that we will one day leave this world, this job, this family, and our children and grandchildren will remain in this world and take over the positive and negative results from our behavior. Healing from sophisticated slavery will make the world a better place with equal rights for all.

8. Use technology for support in healing from sophisticated slavery. Use your phone to help record police misconduct and any other abuse you see in your community.

9. Family System – is one main area that everyone can help in healing from sophisticated slavery. The African American family was destroyed in the past. They are still healing to this day. Divorce rates are high in African American families.

   Church used to be the main source of support but currently African American families do not attend church the way they used to due to work, divorce and other factors.

   The spiritual lives of African American families were tied into attend church during the week, returning back on Sunday to praise and for fellowship. That system is broken and not as strong as before.

10. Financial System – African Americans in past, as slaves, were not paid. They used to stay on the plantation grounds with the entire family. It is very sad to say that African Americans in new jobs, salaries' vary from extremely high to extremely low. Pay should be equal to men and women depending on their experience and education, not the color of their skin.

11. Health Care System - There should be healthcare for everyone, white, black, elderly, or young individuals, any pre-existing condition should be covered by health care in the United States. Thank God for Obama Care that helped everyone have health care. This is a benefit that every person should have. Our body is the temple of God.

12. Prison Systems – Past slavery was already a prison. However, today in recent sophisticated slavery a large majority of African American people are housed within the prison system.

    If you review the statistics most African American people are in prison for much longer prison sentences then Caucasian people *for the same crime*. This is a system that should be reviewed and changed to become fair and equal to all people.

13. It would be a great point of healing for all people gathered together to start healing the world, such as sports, concerts, and corporate events, just to name a few. Everyone should take part in some kind of healing practice or exercise, getting to know someone different from you.. Healing creates a safe place to share differences, share new cultural awareness and keep this as a part of healing and growing out of sophisticated slavery.

African American Men in the Mass Incarceration System

CHAPTER ONE

African American Men in the Mass Incarceration System

African American men are being killed and placed in prison systems at an alarming rate. It's a good time to reflect on ways we can avoid going to prison. Mass incarceration is the modern-day slavery. The numbers of African American men today is equivalent to African American men that were slaves. We are looking for ways to help African American men to stay out of prison. Here are 10 suggestions and positive tools on how African American men can avoid the trap of incarceration, which can help them move out of the sophisticated slavery system.

1. Get involved in the community. Attempt to locate productive, positive programs and organizations that you can get involved in. Parks, community centers or city programs can be a place to look.

2. Get involved in sports. Join a neighborhood sports team, basketball, football or baseball. There are many community leagues a person can join.

3. Get involved in your spiritual community, a church, a mosque or a temple. Whatever your religion is get connected and involved. Locate one that may have a men's or a prison ministry.

4. Be around older African men that are a positive influence. Often older men have learned from bad decisions and poor life choices. They can provide wisdom on how they could have handled situations you are going through differently.

5. Change your negative environment into a positive environment. It is hard to change in a positive direction if you are still surrounded by negative influences. Find new circle of friends that are doing positive things. Avoid the old crowd you hung around that can be a negative influence, or does not support the positive changes you are trying to make.

6. Be open to a new positive lifestyle. Even though it may be different from the type of life you are living. Be open to positive change. Try to eliminate bad behavior, and bad habits. Be responsible, take care of your household. Make an effort to do the necessary things you weren't doing before.

7. Focus on your family and raising your children. Children learn by example and need both parents in the household. A child's foundation is developed in the first ten years. Having a father present is a crucial element to their successful development. Do everything you can to raise your child in a healthy way. Especially if there wasn't a father present in your life. Do not continue the cycle of not having a father in the household.

8. Learn new positive ways to manage anger. Life can be frustrating, but anger can be managed in a positive manner. Learn activities that help you relieve stress and frustration, such as playing basketball, video games, watching sports, boxing, fishing. There are so many constructive things you can do to avoid trouble.

9. Avoid drugs and drinking alcohol. Living in a stressful, unhealthy environment can be easy to turn to drugs or alcohol to escape life. Drugs and alcohol have destroyed the African American community. Alcoholism and other addictions can be hereditary.

10. End and avoid all illegal activities. Violence, gang activity, robbery, drug dealing, trafficking, physical and sexual assault only lead to one of two things death or prison. Choose life even though it may be easier to do the wrong thing, or it may be all you are used to. Choose an alternative way of life to be alive and present for your family, the community and whatever you have to offer the world.

Please take some time to journal for Personal Introspection.

Also, take some time to discuss your thoughts with a friend, church pastor, counselor, therapist or psychiatrist then journal your thoughts.

Personal Introspection

_____

_____

_____

Talk to a friend

_____

_____

_____

Talk to a church pastor

_____

_____

_____

Talk to a counselor or therapist

_____

_____

_____

Talk to a psychiatrist to prescribe medication if needed with counseling

_____

_____

_____

CHAPTER TWO

Education

CHAPTER TWO

Effectively utilize Education

One way to heal from sophisticated slavery is to become educated. In the past and still today a lack of education is used to leave the African American population behind. It has been used as a way to keep African Americans in bondage through illiteracy or a lack of education. Now that everyone is entitled to an education, it is important to seize the opportunity to get an education. Instead of being segregated by color, the education system is segregated by class. The lower your income the lower level of education you will receive.

Often African Americans in low-income neighborhoods do not receive a quality education, or the school has severe behavior issues because it is in a bad neighborhood. Elementary school is the most essential part of a child's educational development. The significance that is placed on a child's education at an early age will determine the passion they have for their education in the future. Creating and supporting a quality education during early childhood will help the child succeed into middle and high school. After high school it is important for a student to find a technical and trade school, associates or bachelor's degree. President Obama is a prime example of how far a quality education can go. Here are some ways you can help your child get the best education so they can achieve academic excellence and have a fair shot in society to overcome sophisticated slavery.

1. Try to enroll children in schools and districts with good ratings. Every school is rated by the state department of education. The better the rating the more money the school receives and the quality of education is better. Vice versa, schools in worse neighborhoods have bad ratings. Depending on the type of neighborhood still seek out the schools that have the better rating.

2. Make sure the school is a safe environment. It is important for every child to have a healthy, safe environment to learn in, even if your child's school isn't in the best neighborhood.

3. Make sure the school is accredited. Some times schools don't have the proper credentials that are required for credits to transfer.

4. Enroll children in Charter or Private schools. Charter schools are a great alternative to Public schools.

5. Home school your children. Home school is an option that is available to any parent.

6. Apply for scholarships. The higher the GPA the more scholarships a student can qualify for. Academic and athletic scholarships are a great way for an intelligent student to get a high quality education at a low cost.

7. Get tutors or assistance for areas that a child is weak in. Often children may be bright but are struggling in a certain area. Instead of thinking the student can't achieve academic excellence in that area, get them help. A tutor can work with them until they clearly understand that subject.

8. Work with the teachers to get the assistance a student needs in areas they are struggling in academically or with their behavior.

9. Get a mentor or positive role model in the student's life. Children learn by example. Find a person that the student can look up to and will be a good influence on them.

Please take some time to journal for Personal Introspection.

Also, take some time to discuss your thoughts with a friend, church pastor, counselor, therapist or psychiatrist then journal your thoughts.

Personal Introspection

_____

_____

_____

Talk to a Friend

_____

_____

_____

Talk to a church pastor

_____

_____

_____

Talk to a counselor or therapist

_____

_____

_____

Talk to a psychiatrist to prescribe medication if needed with counseling

_____

_____

_____

CHAPTER THREE

Health

CHAPTER THREE

Health

I have heard from several spiritual people and elders that the body is the temple of God. Each of us were created in a special way each of us. We have different physical shapes and sizes. We have different skin color and shades.

It is important to keep the body in good condition.

We must first seek medical care once we see any changes to our body. A medical doctor can advise you if something needs special attention. It is just as important to seek a mental and spiritual Counselor in cases when you feel areas of your life are changing, or when you do not understand and do not know what to do.

Fear of the unknown seems to happen when human beings don't seek the proper health care they need. It is important to keep your heath in good, excellent condition.

Rest is an important factor to keep our body in excellent mental and physical shape. It varies from person to person, however, consult your doctor to make sure you have the correct amount of sleep you need every night. This will ensure alert and excellent awareness for the next day.

The Mayo clinic has a recommended amount of sleep listed below for every age.

Newborns 14 to 17 hours a day

12 months About 10 hours at night, plus 4 hours of naps

2 years About 11 to 12 hours at night, plus a 1- to 2-hour afternoon nap

3 to 5 years 10 to 13 hours

6 to 13 years 9 to 11 hours

14 to 17 years 8 to 10 hours

Adults 7 to 9 hours

A massage is something not often communicated in our adult lifestyle, however, it is important to have your skin and body massaged. It can be a costly expense, however, it will pay off in the long run with excellent health. A massage will help you to relax and help heal your spirit. Another key factor is it will help reduce stress.

Stress, as it connects to health is something we are ashamed to communicate about in our culture, since we work 8 hours or more a day, or attend school or college. It is something we do not want to communicate about for fear of sounding weak or vulnerable.

Often, people do not know how to handle stress. If stress is not controlled properly it will affect your work, family life, and other areas in your life.

Please take some time to journal for Personal Introspection.

Also, take some time to discuss your thoughts with a friend, church pastor, counselor, therapist or psychiatrist then journal your thoughts.

Personal Introspection

_____

_____

_____

Talk to a friend

_____

_____

_____

Talk to a church pastor

_____

_____

_____

Talk to a counselor or therapist

_____

_____

_____

Talk to a psychiatrist to prescribe medication if needed with counseling

_____

_____

_____

CHAPTER FOUR

Employment

CHAPTER FOUR

Employment

Work is the key to having a successful career or business. I have been working since I was thirteen. I paid half my mother's mortgage since I was seventeen. I know the value of work and how important it is to life.

Finding your passion is the key to a successful work life. Finding your passion as early as possible is also a key factor. You can research what your passions are by consulting Human Resources for an assessment. When you are in college you can narrow down your career passions by the academic course load you select and enjoy.

I located my passion in church. We had a course called New Members class. It identified all the strengths a person has, which was also very helpful for me in locating my careers as a counselor, writer and advisor.

Once you locate the employment you enjoy it is important to start good work habits and routines, such as going to work every day, on time. Your job will pay for your education if you have a company with that benefit. Your job will pay for your basic needs, such as a place to live and a car to drive. Your job will pay for great trips to see the world if you choose.

Be very focused and present on the task at hand while you are at work. Longevity is important on a job, to have good benefits for the present as well as your future retirement

African American people need to know the importance of networking with friends and family if you want to move up in a company. Most positions are offered by word of mouth in most corporations. Do your best to network with co-workers and other groups in the corporation to make sure you stay open to opportunities. I was in my fifties when I figured out this key secret to corporate America; Networking. Who you know is the key to locating employment or your next dream job. Please keep that in mind on your employment journey.

In the African American culture the focus is just to survive, saving for the future or saving for retirement is rarely talked about. If you do not have a trust fund or if you do not have parents that save for their children's futures or if they do not treat all siblings the same, you must make sure you have a plan for retirement.

Please take some time to journal for Personal Introspection.

Also, take some time to discuss your thoughts with a friend, church pastor, counselor, therapist or psychiatrist then journal your thoughts.

Personal Introspection

_____

_____

_____

Talk to a friend

_____

_____

_____

Talk to a church pastor

_____

_____

_____

Talk to a counselor or therapist

_____

_____

_____

Talk to a psychiatrist to prescribe medication if needed with counseling

_____

_____

_____

CHAPTER FIVE

Physical Abuse

CHAPTER FIVE

Physical Abuse

Physical Abuse is something that some people think is normal. Like me for example, in my past as a child.

All I would see is my father beat my mother, and we children were beaten as well. It was a daily way of life, even if you did not do anything wrong. So as a child and young adult, one grows up to believe that is the way a man is supposed to treat a woman.

Let me start off by saying this is not correct. No one in this world deserves to be beaten. No one in this world deserves violence in any shape, form, or fashion.

Please be aware of the signs of anger, at home, at work or in your relationships with others.

Be aware, if you are relating with a person in any relationship that has excessive verbal fighting, it can sometimes move into physical violence.

Feel free to tell a friend, family member, or neighbor if you see signs of any abuse at any time.

If a pattern of threats of harm to you or anyone you know continue it is important to tell someone right away.

If you feel that physical abuse is something you even feel *may* happen it is important to seek counsel right away.

Early prevention of violence is the key to having a healthy relationship.

If you do not feel safe sharing this secret with a close family member or friend, seek a community support group.

Self-defense is something I encourage everyone to have. Seek a self-defense class. Learn martial arts. Learn how to carry mace. Educate yourself by taking a gun safety class at your local gun shop.

Any way you feel safe that is best for you is important. I have a permit to carry. I have basic training in how to carry a gun and protect myself.

I have never had to use it, however, I feel safe with knowing and understanding safety rules, policies and procedures.

Find which self-defense techniques make you feel safe

So many African American men are killed daily, weekly and monthly without any consequences to their killers. I feel sorry for the African American men that are killed and not justified by law. I feel sorry for the way African American men are physically and mentally abused by society.

I hope this worksheet can help you with options in the case of Physical Abuse.

Please take some time to journal for Personal Introspection.

Also, take some time to discuss your thoughts with a friend, church pastor, counselor, therapist or psychiatrist then journal your thoughts.

Personal Introspection

_____

_____

_____

Talk to a friend

_____

_____

_____

Talk to a church pastor

_____

_____

_____

Talk to a counselor or therapist

_____

_____

_____

Talk to a psychiatrist to prescribe medication if needed with counseling

_____

_____

_____

CHAPTER SIX

Sexual Abuse

CHAPTER SIX

Sexual Abuse

I would like to encourage all women with sons and daughters to be mindful of sexual abuse. It can happen right within your family. With a family member you trust, love and adore. Please protect your children from sexual abuse by being open and letting a child know about their bodies very early in life, as early as you and your doctor feel they can understand. This may vary from child to child depending on their maturity level.

Your doctor is very open to advise you. Hopefully you will be open to the conversation. Teaching your child about appropriate touch is very important in your child's healthy upbringing.

If your child has been sexually abused, it is important to see a doctor and your local police right away. Have the sexual abuse documented with your family doctor.

One of the key problems within African American households is keeping secrets. Unclear communications break down African American families. The shame in the family is a huge part of the culture. It is important to talk about sex in every stage of your children's life. Remove the fear and stigma about sex.

It is a part of life. It is a part of all cultures. It is something that should be shared in church, schools and in all families. So if the open conversation is not occurring at home, maybe the church or school can support and educate the kids on what is appropriate and what is not.

African American women in past slavery were sexually abused by the slave masters. Currently in every industry women are communicating openly about sexual abuse and all inequality. It's time for all women to start talking to each other on ways to heal, break the shame, and start protecting each other. It hurts me to know that women do not believe other women when they've been sexually or physically damaged.

Please take some time to journal for Personal Introspection.

Also, take some time to discuss your thoughts with a friend, church pastor, counselor, therapist or psychiatrist then journal your thoughts.

Personal Introspection

_____

_____

_____

Talk to a friend

_____

_____

_____

Talk to a church pastor

_____

_____

_____

Talk to a counselor or therapist

_____

_____

_____

Talk to a psychiatrist to prescribe medication if needed with counseling

_____

_____

_____

CHAPTER SEVEN

Find Your Purpose

CHAPTER SEVEN

Find Your Purpose

A way to heal from sophisticated slavery is to discover your purpose in life. African Americans are very innovative and artistically creative. They have always been leaders in entertainment, professional sports, education, politics and inventions. Everyone has a special gift and talent. As a person discovers their passion and purpose they can become more successful. Eventually a person can turn their passion into a form of income. Think of ways that you can use your creativity and innovation to make money, then over time, your part time passion can become your full time passion. The greatest freedom is to be able to create something out of nothing.

Take a dream and build it into a lucrative empire. During segregation there were so many entrepreneurs because African Americans had no choice but to shop at the neighborhood grocer, barber or locksmith that was owned and operated by African Americans. Now, it is much easier for African Americans to become entrepreneurs the same mentality should apply.

A way to heal from sophisticated slavery is by creating and sustaining an economy by African American entrepreneurs. Here are some helpful tips on how you can discover your purpose.

1. Discover a talent or gift that you have. Your passion is something that you are extraordinarily good at and that brings you joy. Everyone has something to offer the world.

2. Find a mentor in the industry of your choice. If you want to become an electrician, look for a mentor who has been an electrician and has many years of experience.

3. Find a passion that you enjoy. Think of something that can help you earn money part-time. Your business may not make you full-time money in the beginning. If you start off part-time then you aren't taking such a huge risk.

   You may not be successful in the beginning. But, keep the faith and keep trying.

4. Get an internship in the career you are interested in. Internships are a great way to learn about a profession. It can give you the chance to try a career out without making the full commitment.

5. Get tutors or assistance for areas that a student is weak in. Often children may be bright but are struggling in a certain area. Instead of thinking the student can't achieve academic excellence in that area, get them help. A tutor can work with them until they clearly understand that subject.

6. Work with teachers to get assistance that a student needs, in areas they are struggling with, such as academics or behavior.

7. Get a mentor or positive role model in the student's life. Children learn by example. Find a person that the student can look up to and will be a good influence.

Please take some time to journal for Personal Introspection.

Also, take some time to discuss your thoughts with a friend, church pastor, counselor, therapist or psychiatrist then journal your thoughts.

Personal Introspection

_____

_____

_____

Talk to a friend

_____

_____

_____

Talk to a church pastor

_____

_____

_____

Talk to a counselor or therapist

_____

_____

_____

Talk to a psychiatrist to prescribe medication if needed with counseling

_____

_____

_____

CHAPTER EIGHT

Retirement

CHAPTER EIGHT

Retirement

Retirement is something not talked about in the young child's life in African American families. I know in my family we never talked about life after work in terms of money, lifestyle, relaxation, ministry, and how to help the community as a whole.

I would like to share information in these areas and hope they give you some insight as you move into the elderly part of your life's journey.

First, money will be the main topic to address.

1. You must work hard. You must save. You must plan early for retirement.

2. Please work with a financial planner. Please work with your Human Resource benefit department.

3. Be open to talk to elders or someone you feel comfortable sharing your long-term goals. This will help you move toward retirement in a more successful manner.

4. It is imperative to pay off credit card debt. Credit cards can be a form of slavery if not used correctly.

So, with all this being said. You must learn to relax after you retire to take off all the years of damage caused by Sophisticated Slavery.

Lifestyle is important.

Drinking, drugs or other bad habits are not good for anyone. These behaviors can abuse your body, mind and spirit. When you retire make sure you become introspective about your lifestyle to have a long time to enjoy retirement.

Most important to me is ministry, plan to do God's or spiritual work that needs to be done in the community, this may vary from person to person. Look into your heart and soul and see if that is important to you.

Please take some time to journal for Personal Introspection.

Also, take some time to discuss your thoughts with a friend, church pastor, counselor, therapist or psychiatrist then journal your thoughts.

Personal Introspection

_____

_____

_____

Talk to a friend

_____

_____

_____

Talk to a church pastor

_____

_____

_____

Talk to a counselor or therapist

_____

_____

_____

Talk to a psychiatrist to prescribe medication if needed with counseling

_____

_____

_____

CHAPTER NINE

Church and Religion

CHAPTER NINE

Church and Religion

It is important to have faith when overcoming adversity. It is important to find out what you love and feel passionate about, it could be in church or religion.

If you are an excellent speaker, singer, or administrative worker, you can find a position at church or spiritual group to fulfill your passion.

One important factor is that you most find something to put your faith and belief in higher than yourself.

It is so important to have faith to overcome sophisticated slavery in belonging to something that you can attend weekly, monthly or yearly that has social interest and bond with other believers just like yourself.

Community involvement is key to healing the world. There are politics, policies that harm people of color every day.

This is not just an African American social interest. This is a human social interest with good will. Everyone can take part in the healing process.

Values of respect and work, family and home-care are important to everyone. To kill and harm any human being is not of good faith and kindness. This must stop and every one of every color has a role to play.

Hardship is a part of life. It will happen if you live a good Christian lifestyle. It will happen no matter how much money you make. Hardship with health, job, and finances, are just a part of life.

It will take everyone to change the old mind-set. It will take every one to participate in every minute, hour, day, week, month in a mind-set of goodwill to each other.

Use patience and kindness to everyone we meet. Use encouragement and love to change and heal the world.

The teaching in church and religion, if used properly, can help heal the world with simple loving techniques. Church and religion are great tools to heal anything broken.

Maintain a spiritual mind-set of peace to every one you meet. Spread healing and positive nonviolence to the world. Church and religion are meant to end wars and violence.

Please take some time to journal for Personal Introspection.

Also, take some time to discuss your thoughts with a friend, church pastor, counselor, therapist or psychiatrist then journal your thoughts.

Personal Introspection

_____

_____

_____

Talk to a friend

_____

_____

_____

Talk to a church pastor

_____

_____

_____

Talk to a counselor or therapist

_____

_____

_____

Talk to a psychiatrist to prescribe medication if needed with counseling

_____

_____

_____

CHAPTER TEN

Love

CHAPTER TEN

Love

Love is an emotion that everyone wants, but it is not easy to find. Love is one of the most important emotions we have as human beings.

African Americans used to have stronger family ties. The African American men loved the African American women so much. He was killed if he ever looked at a Caucasian woman.

The focus for an African American man was strong because he gave the African American woman 100% of his love, when he was not working in the cotton fields, or working on the field house when his chores were assigned.

Times have changed. To court someone in this day and time and generation you have a computer or phone line to connect with another human being. Online dating, speed dating, chat lines for dating and other ways to connect are endless.

The divorce rate of African American families is high. The value for African American families to stay connected and together has changed.

African American women deserve more respect, more kindness, and more patience. This is also a need for the African American men.

I am here to spread the word that love is the most important thing you show and give to people and animals in your life.

I have learned that the more I love God and trust God, love is much easier to understand and give.

Please take some time to journal for Personal Introspection.

Also, take some time to discuss your thoughts with a friend, church pastor, counselor, therapist or psychiatrist then journal your thoughts.

Personal Introspection

_____

_____

_____

Talk to a friend

_____

_____

_____

Talk to a church pastor

_____

_____

_____

Talk to a counselor or therapist

_____

_____

_____

Talk to a psychiatrist to prescribe medication if needed with counseling

_____

_____

_____

Jealousy And Forgiveness

CHAPTER ELEVEN

Jealousy and Forgiveness

The main reason I would like to discuss these two topics together is because they work hand in hand. If you feel jealousy or envy of any human being, that will make your treatment of them non-caring, non-loving, and disrespectful. This is a major concern in the African American community. African American people from past slavery often feel they have less in many areas. I would love to name those areas to you in detail. They feel they lack in the areas of employment, housing, status, and varies aspects of life. This can create jealousy and envy of anyone put in opportunities that are better than what they have received.

This is a common, daily, weekly, monthly experience I would love you to become introspective of and beware of how you're using that mistreated behavior. If not, that jealousy and envy can change your spiritual energy if you're not aware of how it's affecting you.

1. It can cause displaced anger to people you love the most who did not cause you harm.

2. It can cause you to use excessive drinking or drugs.

3. It can cause you to lash out in a violent manner.

4. It can silence you with inward pain and cause internal medical problems.

5. It can cause you to stutter and not speak clearly.

6. It can cause you to come home angry and not show love and kindness to your family in a proper manner.

7. It can cause you to have low self esteem and devalue the beauty that is within you. Without truly understanding the external effect of what this is doing to your mind, body and spirit.

8. Please do not compare yourself to others. African American people please honor your skin color, your hair, your talent, and embrace your African American women with love and admiration.

Please take some time to journal for Personal Introspection.

Also, take some time to discuss your thoughts with a friend, church pastor, counselor, therapist or psychiatrist then journal your thoughts.

Personal Introspection

_____

_____

_____

Talk to a friend

_____

_____

_____

Talk to a church pastor

_____

_____

_____

Talk to a counselor or therapist

_____

_____

_____

Talk to a psychiatrist to prescribe medication if needed with counseling

_____

_____

_____

Please Pray for the African American Grandmothers

CHAPTER TWELVE

Please pray for the African American Grandmothers

Due to the massive killings of the African American male, and a large majority of African American incarceration the African American grandmother has been the savior of our culture.

1. African American grandmothers have stepped in to heal the family after it's been broken and help raise the grandkids.

2. The African American grandmother role has changed from being an elder to being an up-front center front-runner parent again.

3. The African American grandmother helps with financial needs, with food daycare, clothing, and in some cases long-term care.

4. It is our duty as a community to pray, support and love grandmothers and elders of the African American culture. Please find ways to support them.

Please take some time to journal for Personal Introspection.

Also, take some time to discuss your thoughts with a friend, church pastor, counselor, therapist or psychiatrist then journal your thoughts.

Personal Introspection

_____

_____

_____

Talk to a friend

_____

_____

_____

Talk to a church pastor

_____

_____

_____

Talk to a counselor or therapist

_____

_____

_____

Talk to a psychiatrist to prescribe medication if needed with counseling

_____

_____

_____

About the Authors:

The authors are two African American women who have experienced sophisticated slavery first hand.

Donna Kay Harris has been an advisor for over eleven years in the academic world. She is the author of three books:

Spiritual Secrets for Successful Single Parenting

Spiritual Poems by Donna Kay Harris

How to Heal from Sophisticated Slavery

Donna has been a gospel singer since the age of five and is a part of the Minnesota State Baptist Convention Choir, We are Better Together in 2016. She has been a member of Pilgrim Baptist Church for over thirty years. She is part of three choirs, Voices of Unity, The Mass Choir and the Praise Team.

Educational background:

Doctor of Education in Leadership Program

Completed coursework toward Doctorate Degree at

Saint Mary's University of Minnesota.

Master of Arts, Alfred Adler Institute of Minnesota, Hopkins, MN

Psychotherapy and Counseling, 1997

Counselor intern at Very Personal Incorporated, St. Paul, MN1994-1997

Co-facilitated group therapy sessions, individual counseling and initiation of individual treatment plans.

Bachelor of Arts, Concordia College, St. Paul, MN, 1992,

Organizational Management and Communication

Her books are a part of her spiritual journey in hopes of inspiring readers and help anyone that needs encouragement.

Leticia Latrice Barrett is the co-author of two books:

"How to Heal from Sophisticated Slavery,"

"Spiritual Secrets for Successful Single Parenting."

Educational background

Leticia Latrice has two master's degrees:

Master's in Business Administration

Master's in Management

Leticia manages multiple businesses. She is the host of the radio show "Let's Talk Life" with Leticia Latrice. Subscribe to the YouTube Channel Letstalklife (all one word). Listen to Let's Talk Life with Leticia Latrice Thursdays at 6:30 pm MST worldwide online at www.radiophoenix.org.

Leticia Latrice is the owner of Prosperous Business Management in a consulting firm that services small businesses. She prepares taxes and is an insurance broker.

Leticia is also an educator and has worked in the Arizona school system as a teacher for the past six years.

Her goal is to inspire and educate the world from her life's experiences.

Printed in the United States
By Bookmasters